WORLD WAR II PEARL HARBOR

A History From Beginning to End

Copyright © 2018 by Hourly History.

All rights reserved.

Table of Contents

Introduction
America Opens the Door to Japan
Pearl Harbor, Home of the Shark Goddess
Air Raid Pearl Harbor, This Is No Drill
The Commanders
The Story of a Survivor
Conclusion

Introduction

As Americans of the 1930s glanced across their Pacific and Atlantic barriers, they found that the insulation afforded by their cushioning oceans suited them just fine. For a nation that had been dealing with unemployment rates of 25%, the Great Depression was enough travail for its citizens to deal with, and the Americans embraced their neutrality. While it was unfortunate that, following the fall of France, Great Britain was left to fight alone against the Nazi aggression and genocide of Adolf Hitler's Germany, it was Europe's battle, and Americans had no wish to take part. On the Pacific side of the nation, Japanese aggression against the Chinese was likewise unfortunate, but Americans wanted no part of someone else's war.

President Franklin D. Roosevelt was no isolationist, and he realized, as the citizens of the nation he had led since 1933 did not, that there would be no shelter from this war. America provided support to Great Britain, Free France, the Republic of China, the Soviet Union, and other Allies through the Lend-Lease program which provided food, oil, and material, including warships, warplanes, and weapons, from 1941 to the end of the war in August 1945. In exchange for the items, the U.S. received leases on army and naval bases located in Allied territory during the war years.

FDR would have liked to do more, but the Neutrality Act of 1939 limited the scope of the assistance that could be offered. American aversion to being engulfed by foreign war required that FDR had to balance his farsighted vision for the conflict with the nearsighted perspective of the nation. With a Gallup poll taken before the war showing that 88% of Americans were against becoming involved in the war in Europe, FDR's 1940 re-election campaign vowed, "I have said this before, but I shall say it again and again and again: Your boys are not going to be sent into any foreign wars."

Americans, when they did think of the war, were aware that the nations in Europe were falling like low-hanging fruit to the Nazis. They knew that Japan had invaded China and seized Manchuria. They were aware that their government was negotiating with the Japanese government, which wanted the U.S. to end the sanctions that were depriving the Japanese of oil and necessary goods. But until December 7, 1941, none of this was sufficient reason for the Americans to enter the war.

That ended when President Roosevelt addressed a joint session of Congress on December 8, the day after the attack. December 7, 1941, was, he declared, a day which would live in infamy. First Lady Eleanor Roosevelt had already prepared the nation for the news in her radio broadcast the night before when she stated, "whatever is asked of us we shall accomplish it; we are the free and unconquerable people of the U.S.A." For his part, her husband regarded the attack on Pearl Harbor as the most serious crisis that any presidential Cabinet had had to deal with since the Civil War.

With only one dissenting vote, Congress voted to go to war against the Empire of Japan an hour after FDR's speech. The dissenting vote was cast by Rep. Jeannette Rankin of Montana. Having flung off its neutrality, the Americans reacted angrily to her pacifism. A mob that followed her as she left the Capitol after her vote forced her to hide in a telephone booth until the Capitol police came to her rescue. America was out for vengeance and was in no mood for peace until it came on American terms.

Germany and Italy declared war against the United States, but America had no more thoughts of avoiding the conflict. The attack on Pearl Harbor was the linchpin to the grenade that launched America into a global conflict for the second time in the twentieth century. But World War II would see a very different result from what World War I had brought, as the United States and its military, rising out of the burning ashes of Pearl Harbor, would emerge as the dominant power, one possessed of a terrible new weapon capable of wreaking destruction on an unfathomable scale.

Chapter One

America Opens the Door to Japan

"Our great state of California produces about sixty millions of dollars in gold every year, besides silver, quicksilver, precious stones, and many other valuable articles. Japan is also a rich and fertile country, and produces many very valuable articles. Your imperial majesty's subjects are skilled in many of the arts. I am desirous that our two countries should trade with each other, for the benefit both of Japan and the United States."

—President Millard Fillmore

To the young American country, Japan was an exotic mystery, one that Commodore Matthew Perry intended to solve. On July 8, 1853, he sailed two frigates and two sailing vessels into Tokyo Bay, seeking to re-establish for the first time in over 200 years regular trade and relations between Japan and the western world. Japan and the west had enjoyed profitable trading relations during the sixteenth and seventeenth centuries until 1639 when the Japanese expelled the foreigners because of what were seen as unfair trade practices and their efforts to convert the Japanese to Catholicism. After that, trade access was granted only to Dutch and Chinese ships which had special charters.

But in the middle of the nineteenth century, Chinese ports were opened to trade from the west. The United States, having acquired California and a Pacific port, wanted to capitalize on trade with Asia. American steamships needed to have coaling stations in order to take on provisions and fuel as they made the long journey to China. There were rumors that Japan had enormous repositories of coal, an enticement which only increased the intention of establishing diplomatic and commercial ties with Japan.

While the whaling trade was still lucrative, the U.S. needed safe harbors in case of shipwrecks. Before Perry's mission, sailors from the U.S. who were shipwrecked were reportedly mistreated by the Japanese. To pacify and persuade the emperor, Perry brought gifts for the Japanese leader, not realizing that the emperor's position was more ceremonial than political and that the actual power was held by the Tokugawa Shogunate. The gifts were intended to prove American superiority and included a working model of a steam locomotive, a telegraph, a telescope, and wines and liquors. He intended to win the government's agreement to protect shipwrecked and stranded ships and to open at least one port for supplies and refueling.

The Japanese were decidedly unenthusiastic, but Perry refused to leave. If the government did not send a suitable representative to receive his letter from President Millard

Fillmore, Perry announced, he himself would deliver the letter and use force if necessary.

Although the harbor was fortified, its defenses were not sufficient to battle Perry. After several days, they accepted his letter from the American president requesting a treaty. The next spring, Perry returned for Japan's answer, and the Treaty of Kanagawa was signed on March 31, 1854. In addition to the sought-after concessions, the treaty included a most-favored-nation clause so that any future concessions granted to other foreign powers would also include the U.S.

In 1856, the first U.S. consul arrived. As he didn't arrive with the naval regalia that Perry brought, the Japanese were not at first amenable to signing a more extended treaty. However, after learning that the British had forced China to open its ports through military action, Japan opted for the diplomatic approach, and in 1858, the first commercial treaty was signed. In 1860, Japan sent a mission to Washington D.C. to ratify the treaty.

Despite its initial reluctance to welcome western trade, Japan utilized the new trade economy to modernize its military and quickly became the chief Asian power in the Pacific. The changes in its commercial role also affected Japanese politics; the Tokugawa Shogunate became weaker, and the Japanese emperor gained formal control of the nation in 1868.

Japan, unlike Europe, was not dragged into the morass of World War I, and the country's industry and trade prospered as Japan filled the gap vacated by the ruined commerce in Europe. But because Japan possessed insufficient natural resources, the nation's manufacturers needed to import raw materials. During the period from 1918 to 1930, as Japan's population surged, the nation could no longer meet the needs of its people. Tariffs imposed on Japanese exports by foreign nations limited the ability of Japan to pay for the food it needed to import.

The crash of the stock market in 1929 and the worldwide Depression affected the Japanese economy just as it devastated so many others in the world. At the same time, the 1930s saw the rise of militarism in Japan. While China had suffered revolution during the 1920s, Japan thought that the northern region of Manchuria, with its wealth of resources, would be the ideal acquisition if Japan wanted to expand its boundaries and solve its internal problems with its population growth.

Acting upon a fabricated terrorist threat, the Kwantung Army seized a city in Manchuria without seeking approval from the Japanese government and without offering proof of its accusations. Despite the efforts of the government to halt the Kwantung Army's aggression, the forces continued to bring Chinese Manchuria under its control. The region was renamed Manchukuo in 1932 as a puppet state of Japan. When China complained to the League of Nations, Japan withdrew from the League, and its armies continued to invade China, stopping just before reaching Peking. The truce that was arranged barred the Chinese from entering the parts of northern China that were occupied by Japan.

By the mid-1930s, Japan was beginning to emerge from the economic shadow of the Great Depression thanks to government deficits that expanded heavy industry and the military. Young men, who had joined the army because the Depression had been so overwhelming in their rural communities, were committed to the idea that they could achieve economic security if they expanded Japan's territory.

By 1937, China and Japan were at war, and while the United States condemned Japan's aggressive behavior, President Franklin D. Roosevelt knew that war with Asia was not a direction favored by the American people still enmeshed in the Great Depression. Americans handled the martial encroachment by refusing to recognize the conquered territory as belonging Japan, imposing economic sanctions against the aggressors and providing military and economic assistance for the Chinese. Japan was insulted by the responses and retaliated by trying to prevent the assistance from reaching China and finding other sources for the items that they could not get from the U.S. due to the sanctions.

As Japan looked upon the landscape of the west, noting the speed and efficiency of Adolf Hitler's military victories, the Asian power reckoned that the French, the British, and the Dutch were incapable of defending the territories those nations controlled in Southeast Asia and the South Pacific. Japan and Germany negotiated an alliance in 1940, and after that, Japan pushed for the French government to allow Japanese troops to occupy northern French Indochina. The next year saw the Japanese occupying all of French Indochina.

As a result, the U.S. increased its economic sanctions. Most threatening was the decision in late summer of 1941 to deny the Japanese the right to purchase any materials, including oil, from the U.S. Japan was almost entirely dependent upon American imports for its oil; if the Japanese didn't have oil, how could they sustain their war against China?

During the latter half of 1941, the two countries were involved in frantic negotiations. If the U.S. would not relent in its sanctions, Japan had only months of oil remaining. Japan decided that if no agreement was reached by the end of November 1941, war was the only option. That war, the Japanese navy realized, would have to be an air strike using carrier-based planes against Pearl Harbor. It would have to be a conclusive attack with the intention of destroying the U.S. Pacific Fleet. If the American naval fleet were lying at the bottom of the ocean, its ships would not be able to impede Japan's plans for domination.

Chapter Two

Pearl Harbor, Home of the Shark Goddess

"When reflecting upon it today, that the Pearl Harbor attack should have succeeded in achieving surprise seems a blessing from Heaven. It was clear that a great American fleet had been concentrated in Pearl Harbor, and we supposed that the state of alert would be very high."

—Hideki Tojo

In the beginning, European explorers like Captain James Cook were not optimistic that Pearl Harbor, because of the coral bar that blocked the entrance, had potential to be a port. But as time went on, that view changed.

The connection between the United States and the Hawaiian Islands had begun during the time when the American whaling industry was booming. In 1846, the peak year for whaling, nearly 800 whaling ships, most of them carrying the American flag, came to Hawaii, whose sugar and pineapple crops were a trade lure. At that time, the American Navy patrolled the islands in order to protect the whaling ships from attack by pirates or other commercial rivals.

The arrival of the westerners galvanized activity in Hawaii, where life had previously gone on as it had for centuries. The cities of Honolulu and Lahaina suddenly were bustling with the influx of sailors. Facilities to repair ships were built. In order to accommodate the new economy, boarding houses appeared, along with laundries, blacksmiths, and other merchants.

But then, in 1859, oil was discovered in Pennsylvania, and with whale oil no longer needed for lamps and fuel, the whaling industry was devastated. What was left was vanquished by the Confederate Navy which sailed deep into the Pacific to chase the remaining whalers and sink them; it wasn't out of vindictiveness, but for the purpose of striking at the economy of the North. As the nineteenth century came to a close, the whaling boom was done. But the Civil War did inspire another trading incentive thanks to the northern boycotting of the southern sugar crop. As imports from Hawaii increased, pineapples became the second-largest export from Hawaii.

Sugar and pineapples were all very well, but the United States was growing, and Hawaii seemed ideal for the establishment of a Pacific port for the American Navy. In 1873, two American military officers traveled secretly to Hawaii to assess the Hawaiian Islands in terms of their defensive capabilities and potential commercial facilities.

Trade, once again, was a dominant factor in relations between the two nations. After the passing of the McKinley Tariff, import rates on foreign sugar increased, resulting in an economic crisis as Hawaiian sugar planters were being undersold in the U.S. market. But the

American sugar growers reasoned that there wouldn't be a tariff on the sugar if the Hawaiian Islands were to be annexed by the U.S.

Hawaii's Queen Liliuokalani did not welcome foreign meddling in her country. That stance was not aligned with the sugar planters, who mounted an uprising in January 1893 and appealed to the American military for protection. Marines, without the approval of the president, stormed the island, and the American flag was raised over Honolulu as the Hawaiian queen was forced to surrender. President Grover Cleveland did not support annexation and instead ordered an investigation into the matter with the intention of restoring the queen to her throne.

But by 1898, the U.S. was at war with Spain, and the Hawaiian Islands had a renewed usefulness as a stopping point en route to the Spanish Philippines. President McKinley signed a resolution annexing Hawaii, which then became an American territory.

According to the native Hawaiians, Pearl Harbor was the home of the shark goddess and her son; the goddess was born of human parents but had changed into a shark. She and her son, legend said, lived in a cave at the entrance to Pearl Harbor and guarded the waters against man-eating sharks. They were friendly gods who protected the fish ponds from intruders, and pearl-producing oysters filled the harbor until late in the 1800s.

By the next century, it was no longer the European explorers who were involving themselves in Pearl Harbor. On December 6, 1884, the United States and the Hawaiian

Kingdom of 1875 signed the Reciprocity Treaty, which gave the U.S. exclusive rights to Pearl Harbor as part of the agreement allowing Hawaii to send its sugar to the U.S. duty-free. As the U.S. flexed its muscle after the Spanish-American War of 1898, the Americans decided that a permanent presence in the Pacific was needed. That led to the decision to annex Hawaii. The channel had to be dredged so that the harbor would be able to accommodate large naval ships, and in 1908, a naval base was created at Pearl Harbor. Within six years, the area around Pearl Harbor would see the establishment of other bases where American marine and army soldiers were housed.

The Hawaiians were less than pleased. When the construction of the first dry dock began in 1909, seismic disturbances caused collapses on the construction site; the Hawaiians believed that the shark god was angry. In order to pacify the angry god, a kahuna was summoned. Years of problems took place over the following decade but finally, in 1919, the first dry dock opened.

Two years before that, Ford Island was purchased for the Army and Navy to use in the development of the military's aviation program. The Pacific was looming as a potential site of conflict; Japan's military and industrial might were expanding, and the U.S.—still a junior player on the world stage but one with the potential to be more—began to keep more ships at Pearl Harbor.

From 1921 to 1940, the United States did not have a two-ocean army. Ships in San Diego and San Francisco were able to quickly deploy if they were needed to defend the Hawaiian Islands or the Panama Canal. But the possibility of war with Japan had been on the American radar screen since the early years of the twentieth century.

The assumption was that if the U.S. and Japan were at war, American bases in the western Pacific would be overrun or blockaded, so the plan was for the U.S. Pacific Fleet to concentrate its might along the western coast. By the 1930s, economic measures had forced naval ships to sail with half of their allotted crew, so time would be needed, if there were an attack, for a full crew to be assembled. The plan was that, after that was accomplished, the ships would sail to relieve the Philippines and then blockade Japan.

In 1932, the Navy participated in a mock attack to explore its defense of Pearl Harbor. For the exercise, Rear Admiral Harry Yarnell was in command of the attacking force. As a naval aviator, one of the few admirals to have this position when battleship command was the path to promotion, Yarnell was instrumental in developing aircraft carrier tactics at a time when carriers were regarding as expendable, good only as fleet scouting elements.

Yarnell's perception was that Japan had always begun its operations by attacking before declaring war, and so his attack plan utilized carrier aviation to launch a surprise attack on Pearl Harbor. The defenders of the harbor expected Yarnell to attack with his battleships, but Yarnell advanced with two carriers north-northeast of Hawaii, and at dawn on February 7, his force of 152 plans launched their attack, first striking the airfields and then the ships.

The defenders were completely caught off guard. Using sacks of white flour to simulate bombs, the mock attacking force scored multiple hits. Not a single plane was able to get airborne as the attack got underway, and the airfields were out of commission. But Yarnell's success and the revelation that Pearl Harbor was vulnerable was not well received by the brass at the Army or Navy. They said that Yarnell, by attacking at dawn on a Sunday morning, had cheated. That was not an appropriate time for an attack, they complained. Attacking from the north-northeast had mimicked planes arriving from the mainland. And, the Navy added, "everyone knew that Asians lacked sufficient hand-eye coordination to engage in that kind of precision bombing" of the battleships at anchor. Under pressure, the exercise umpires who had credited Yarnell with winning the exercise reversed their decision under pressure from the War Department.

The admirals refused to believe that Pearl Harbor was susceptible to attack by naval air power. The Japanese were paying attention to the coverage of the exercise that was reported in the press, and in fact, the exercise was observed by Japanese naval officers who were at the Japanese consulate on Oahu. What the American naval brass refused to consider remained in the thoughts of the Japanese who would imitate Yarnell's attack a decade later, with six carriers and twice the air power that Yarnell used.

But the military did not fail to notice the strategic value of Pearl Harbor. In 1935, the Army spent $15 million to build Hickam Field, a new base for its Air

Corps station in the Pacific. The thirties saw the shadows of war loom across Europe, but discerning eyes could tell that the conflict would not allow the Pacific to be disengaged. The U.S., although still neutral after France and Great Britain went to war against Germany in 1939, decided to hold its fleet exercise in 1940 in Hawaii. On February 1, 1941, the Americans divided its naval resources into separate Atlantic and Pacific fleets, with the Pacific Fleet permanently lodged at Pearl Harbor.

Just as the Japanese had been watching in 1932 as the United States conducted its mock attack exercises on Pearl Harbor, they were watching now. They observed as the Americans made more improvements to the channel so that, by the middle of 1941, the entire American Pacific Fleet could be berthed within Pearl Harbor. What seemed like a move for convenience to the Americans would prove to be a golden opportunity for the Japanese and their plans to control the Pacific by knocking out the American Navy.

Chapter Three

Air Raid Pearl Harbor, This Is No Drill

"Indeed, one hour after Japanese air squadrons had commenced bombing in the American island of Oahu, the Japanese ambassador to the United States and his colleague delivered to our Secretary of State a formal reply to a recent American message. And while this reply stated that it seemed useless to continue the existing diplomatic negotiations, it contained no threat or hint of war or of armed attack."

—President Franklin Delano Roosevelt

The year 1941 was one of intense negotiations between the United States and its Pacific rival, but President Roosevelt had rejected Japanese concessions, despite their willingness to withdraw from most of China and French Indochina after peace with the Nationalist government was made. Before he would agree to meet with the Japanese prime minister, President Roosevelt wanted an agreement. The American ambassador to Japan had alerted FDR that the only way to achieve peace was to meet with the prime minister, but FDR was adamant. An agreement before a meeting, or no meeting.

The next month, the government of Japan collapsed upon the refusal by the Japanese military to withdraw from China. On November 20, the Japanese offered to withdraw from southern Indochina and to not attack in Southeast Asia if the Americans, Dutch, and British would end their sanctions against Japan and stop providing aid to the Chinese. The Americans had a counterproposal which was delivered on November 27, 1941, but it was already too late; the Japanese attack fleet had left for Pearl Harbor on November 26.

The six aircraft carriers intended to use 408 aircraft in the attack.

On December 7, the U.S. Army radar picked up the arrival of the first wave of the Japanese attack, but the post, although in training for six months, was not operational and there was disagreement regarding what was approaching. Six B-17 bombers were scheduled to arrive from California, and the officer at the post disagreed with the operators who called the approach a target. The Japanese were approaching at a very few degrees of difference from the bombers, and the operators neglected to tell their officer of the size of the advancing force.

At 7:48 am Hawaiian Time, the air attack began. The 353 planes reached Oahu in two waves. The torpedo bombers attacked the battleships while the dive bombers struck the bases of Hickam Field and Wheeler Field on Oahu. During the second wave, 171 planes attacked the Army Air Force Base at Bellows Field and Ford Island. The only aerial opposition that the Americans mounted came from a handful of P-36 Hawks, P-40 Warhawks, and some SBD Dauntless dive bombers from the aircraft carrier USS *Enterprise*.

Not expecting an attack, the American sailors scrambled at the message "Air Raid Pearl Harbor. This is no drill" from the headquarters of Patrol Wing Two, the first senior Hawaiian command that responded. They found that their ammunition lockers were locked. Guns were unmanned. On a leisurely Sunday morning, no one was expecting to need guns or ammunition.

The 90-minute attack left 2,008 sailors, 218 soldiers and airmen, 109 marines, and 68 civilians dead. Eighteen ships, including five battleships, had either been sunk or run aground. Half of the American deaths were caused by the explosion of the forward magazine on the USS *Arizona* after it was hit by a modified 16-inch shell from a Nakajima B5N torpedo bomber. As the USS *Nevada*, which was on fire from a torpedo hit, tried to escape from the harbor, the Japanese bombers sent bombs to prevent the ship from getting away. To prevent the *Nevada* from blocking the entrance to the harbor, the ship was intentionally beached. After the USS *California* was hit by two bombs and two torpedoes, the crew was ordered to abandon ship. The USS *Utah*, a disarmed target ship, was hit by torpedoes. The seventh torpedo that hit the USS *West Virginia* tore the ship's rudder. The USS *Oklahoma* capsized after the last two of the four torpedoes to hit the ship struck above the belt armor. The USS *Maryland*, although hit by two 16-inch shells converted into bombs, was not seriously damaged.

In addition to hitting the battleships, the Japanese struck other vessels as well, including light cruisers, destroyers, a repair vessel, and a seaplane tender. The devastation overall was terrible; of the 402 American aircraft, 188 were destroyed, 159 were damaged. Few of the aircraft had been ready to defend the base, and 155 of those damaged were on the ground.

Eight Army Air Force pilots got airborne while the attack was underway, and one Japanese aircraft was brought down. Several American planes were brought down by friendly fire. In addition, three of the nine civilian planes flying in the area were shot.

All the battleships except for the *Arizona* and the *Oklahoma* were repaired and were able to return to service. Fortunately, the three aircraft carriers that had been sent from Pearl Harbor were not victims of the attack and would be able to serve in their intended capacity. But on the day of the attack, there was no hopeful news. The billowing smoke from the attack covered Pearl Harbor, and the ships were monuments to the efficiency of the Japanese bombing.

American intelligence had failed. Expecting Japan to attack the European colonies that were closer than Pearl Harbor, which was 4,000 miles away, the military had failed to defend its base. That meant that almost all of the Pacific Fleet was in the harbor, with hundreds of planes at the airfields nearby.

The intelligence experts were, however, right about Japan's plans to attack the European colonies. Ninety minutes before the attack on Pearl Harbor got underway, the Japanese invaded British Malaya, the New Territories of Hong Kong, Wake Island, the Philippines, and Thailand.

Because these attacks took place on the opposite side of the dateline, the attack happened on December 8, 1941. Regardless of the calendar, the effect was numbing. Reasoning that, by destroying America's Pacific Fleet, the United States would be powerless to retaliate, Japan was sure that it would be free to conquer the South Pacific. The Japanese assumed that, after destroying so many American vessels and airplanes, along with dry docks and airfields, with a staggering count of 2,403 sailors and civilians killed and more than 1,000 wounded, their plan had been executed flawlessly.

But that would not be the case. Aircraft carriers and not battleships were now the most significant naval vessels on the oceans, and none of the Pacific Fleet's carriers were on the base that day, some delivering troops to Wake and Midway Islands, others having returned to the mainland. The Japanese, by failing to strike at the onshore oil storage depots, shipyards, submarine docks, and repair shops, could not prevent the Navy from getting back in order fairly quickly.

American outrage, too, was of enormous impact. The Office of War Information quickly stoked the indignation of the country, inspiring patriotism on the home front. Responding to the rallying cry of "Remember Pearl Harbor," Americans switched, seemingly overnight, to a wartime economy and a wartime frame of mind. By the end of 1941, America had 1.8 million men in the military.

By the end of 1942, that number had risen to 3.9 million and by 1943, 9.1 million. Of those 9.1 million, 38% or 3 million were volunteering their services. As American men donned their country's uniform and went overseas to fight the enemy, American women filled their places in the factories, working at jobs previously performed by men so that the nation's accelerated pace of industry would not slacken.

When Winston Churchill learned of the attack on Pearl Harbor, the prime minister of the beleaguered British immediately realized what this meant. He had been despondent over his nation's prospects for victory. But Pearl Harbor changed everything "So, we had won after all! . . . We had won the war. England would live; Britain would live. . . . How long the war would last or in what fashion it would end no man could tell, nor did I at this moment care . . . We should not be wiped out. Our history would not come to an end. We might not even have to die as individuals. Hitler's fate was sealed. Mussolini's fate was sealed. As for the Japanese, they would be ground to powder. All the rest was merely the proper application of overwhelming force."

He was four years premature with his optimistic prediction, but he was correct in his intuition that the entry of the United States into the war would be the turning point that would ultimately lead to Allied victory.

Chapter Four

The Commanders

"I feel that a surprise attack (submarine, air, or combined) on Pearl Harbor is a possibility, and we are taking immediate practical steps to minimize the damage inflicted and to ensure that the attacking force will pay."

—Admiral Husband E. Kimmel

In 1915, Husband Kimmel was assigned as an aide to Franklin Delano Roosevelt, who was then the Assistant Secretary of the Navy under President Woodrow Wilson. Kimmel had graduated from the United States Naval Academy in 1904, and from there he went on to serve in the Caribbean on battleships. When the United States occupied Veracruz, Mexico, Kimmel was part of the occupation force and was wounded in 1914.

He served during World War I as a squadron gunnery officer as part of the Sixth Battle Squadron of the British Grand Fleet. Following the conclusion of the war, Kimmel was the Executive Officer aboard the USS *Arkansas* and commanded two destroyer divisions. After completing the senior course at the Naval War College, he was given the rank of captain in 1926. The next decade saw him hold a number of different Navy Department assignments along with commanding a destroyer squadron and the USS *New*

York, a battleship. Promoted to the flag rank of rear admiral in 1937, he was named Cruiser Division Seven commander on a diplomatic cruise to South America.

By the time World War II broke out, he was a rear admiral in command of the cruiser forces at Pearl Harbor. In May 1940, the new home for the fleet was Pearl Harbor instead of its former base at San Diego, California. James Richardson, commander of the Pacific Fleet, objected to basing the fleet at Pearl Harbor, believing that it made the fleet too vulnerable to attack, and when President Roosevelt relieved him of duty, Kimmel took Richardson's place. On February 18, 1941, Kimmel informed Admiral Harold Rainsford Stark, Chief of Naval Operations, that, given the possibility of a surprise attack on Pearl Harbor, steps were being taken immediately to address the issue.

Regarded as a diligent and hard worker who inspired the men under him, he was also credited with imbuing the fleet with efficiency and training. "Bull" Halsey, who would become a five-star fleet admiral during the war, regarded Kimmel as ideal for the position. Despite the praise of officers like Halsey, others later accused Kimmel of being a slave to detail; they said that he was prone to overanalyzing tasks that he had already done instead of delegating them. Others said that he was lacking in insight and imagination, too reliant on traditional methods and too inclined to follow routine.

The Japanese were in Washington D.C. negotiating, and rumors were rife that the Japanese intended to attack, but Kimmel believed that an attack would take place at Wake Island or Midway Island, not Pearl Harbor. His request for extra antiaircraft artillery for support from Pearl Harbor for Wake Island was not answered because support could not be spared. In April 1941, Kimmel requested additional resources to build the base at Wake Island; he also asked to have a Marine defense battalion stationed there. The first permanent Marine garrison was assigned to Wake Island in August. He ordered Marine fighters and pilots to Wake Island in November, and on December 5, he sent the USS *Lexington* from Pearl Harbor with the assignment to ferry Marine dive bombers to Midway. Those missions away from Pearl Harbor meant that when the attack came, neither the USS *Enterprise* nor the USS *Lexington* was at Pearl Harbor.

When the Japanese began their attack on Pearl Harbor, Kimmel witnessed the terrible destruction. Watching from the window of his office at the submarine base, Kimmel was wounded with a spent bullet that cut him. Kimmel responded to the minor injury by noting that, "It would have been merciful had it killed me." An aide who was standing beside Kimmel throughout the attack recalled years later that as Kimmel watched the destruction of the fleet, he tore off his four-star shoulder boards, knowing that the attack heralded the end of his command.

After the attack was assessed, Kimmel's predictability was regarded as one of the reasons that the Pacific Fleet was so vulnerable and unprepared, even though the possibility of a Japanese attack was not unknown. On December 17, Kimmel was relieved of command of the Pacific Fleet. A commission appointed by President

Roosevelt determined that Kimmel was guilty of dereliction of duty in the days before the attack. Kimmel's decision to retire from the Navy in January 1942 may have avoided a court-martial despite Kimmel's defense that he had not been provided with important information. Kimmel would later blame FDR for the damage to his naval career, believing that Roosevelt knew that the Japanese were going to bomb Pearl Harbor.

Isoroku Yamamoto, the Japanese naval officer who planned the attack on Pearl Harbor, had graduated from the Japanese naval academy in 1904 and worked in Washington D.C. as a naval attaché at the Japanese embassy from 1926 to 1927. His career prospered, and by August 1941, he was commander-in-chief of Japan's Combined Fleet. Yamamoto did not support war with the United States, concerned that a prolonged war with the Americans would not serve Japan's long-term interests. However, after the government decided that war was the correct response, Yamamoto decided that the only option that would work would be to attack Pearl Harbor by surprise and destroy the U.S. Pacific forces. There was a caveat, however; if the war with the U.S. lasted longer than a year, Yamamoto said that the Japanese would lose.

Yamamoto's intention was for the attack to begin 30 minutes after Japan announced that its peace negotiations with the U.S. had ended. The notification was sent to the Japanese Embassy in Washington D.C., but the transcription took too much time for the ambassador to deliver it according to schedule. Actually, the United States codebreakers had already translated the bulk of the message. Japanese newspapers published a declaration of war on December 8, but this was not delivered to the U.S. until after the attack.

The controversy over whether or not Japan attacked without a declaration of war has continued since 1941, but in 1999, a Japanese professor of law and international relations found documents attesting to the debate within the Japanese government on the subject. What he found was that the Japanese military did not want to give prior notice that the negotiations had come to an end or that war was to be declared. The actual message was not, in any case, a definite declaration; the last paragraph only read, "The Japanese Government regrets to have to notify hereby the American Government that in view of the attitude of the American Government it cannot but consider that it is impossible to reach an agreement through further negotiations."

Yamamoto's planning was masterful. Within 30 minutes of the attack, several American battleships were capsized, destroyed or immobilized, 180 aircraft destroyed, and thousands dead and wounded. The Japanese rejoiced in the resounding success of the raid, but Yamamoto was seen to be less sanguine.

While the staff celebrated the success of the attack, Yamamoto spent the day in depression. He disapproved of the fact that the attack took place while the two countries were at peace. The sneak attack, he knew, would infuriate the Americans and galvanize them into retaliation. He is reputed to have said, "I fear we have awakened a sleeping giant and filled him with a terrible resolve." Historians, however, are dubious that Yamamoto made the statement. The quotation was first uttered as dialogue in the movie *Tora! Tora! Tora!*, a 1970s film about the Pearl Harbor attack. According to historian Steve Gillon, "As far as I know, we have no evidence that Yamamoto ever made the observation following the attack that Japan had awakened a sleeping giant," The film's director and producer countered that although Yamamoto did not utter the quote, he wrote it in his diary.

Whether or not the quotation was actually attributed to Yamamoto, the prediction was accurate. By June 1942, at the Battle of Midway, when the Japanese Navy lost four aircraft carriers along with many planes and pilots, their naval forces were dealt a death blow.

Yamamoto himself was killed in 1943 when American forces ambushed his plane over Bougainville Island and shot him down.

Chapter Five

The Story of a Survivor

"Never a day goes by for all these many years when I haven't thought about it. I don't talk about it too much, but when December rolls around I do. It's important the American people don't forget."

—Donald Stratton

Eighteen-year-old Donald Stratton's days on the USS *Arizona* were spent scraping and cleaning the boats: two 50-foot motorboats, two 40-foot launches, whaleboats, the admiral's barge on the boat deck, and the captain's deck. The USS *Arizona*, which had been commissioned in 1916, weighed 31,000 tons and was home to over 1,700 men. It was refitted in January 1941, and Donald Stratton and the rest of the crew sailed for Hawaii on January 23. The U.S. Pacific Fleet had been moved to Pearl Harbor, Hawaii from San Pedro, California in May of 1940.

The eight battleships, three aircraft carriers, and numerous cruisers, destroyers, and smaller craft took up their new home in Pearl Harbor as evidence of America's nautical might. For Stratton, who had enlisted in Nebraska, the lush green of Hawaii was a very different scene from his Dust Bowl home. Life aboard ship wasn't glamorous, but for a young man who saw no opportunity at home, the Navy offered something more. Daily duties included practicing firing and loading the ship's armament; the shells weighed between 70 and 80 pounds. Stratton's job was as sight setter for the gun. At the time, Stratton didn't recall any thoughts about war on Japan. But when he and the others were sent on maneuvers and were only allowed five gallons of water daily, the men realized that there had to be a reason why they were learning how to adapt in the event that water would one day be rationed.

On the morning of December 7, 1941, Stratton went to breakfast around 7:00 am after reveille and clean-up. It was a Sunday, and the crew, except for the Marines and the boat crew, was mainly dressed in shorts and tee-shirts. When breakfast ended, Stratton headed to the sickbay to visit a friend who was ill. It was around 8:00 am, and he had just stepped out of the mess area when he heard other sailors yelling and pointing at Ford Island. As one of the towers on Ford Island fell, Stratton saw planes bearing the symbol of the Rising Sun fly off, followed by bombs exploding.

Realizing that this wasn't a drill, Stratton headed for his battle station, one deck above the bridge. His job was to crank the orders from the gunnery officer into a gauge and then send the estimated coordinates to the gun crew. After the coordinates were set, the crew would switch the gun to automatic. There wasn't time to think; Stratton immediately went into action. As they fired at the high-altitude bombers, Stratton and others realized that their shells were bursting before they reached the altitude where they would have been able to hit their targets.

The USS *Arizona* was hit on top of the Number 3 turret, but the bomb bounced over the side of the ship. Another went through the afterdeck but didn't explode. Ten minutes after the attack began, the *Arizona* was hit by an 800-kg armor-piercing bomb that penetrated the deck of the ship and exploded in the forward powder magazine. The blast gutted the ship. The foremast and forward superstructure began collapsing.

Stratton recalled that the explosion was enormous and raised the ship nearly out of the water and then back down again. A ball of flame rose more than 500 feet in the air, engulfing the entire foremast and the bow of the ship. "It just rattled us around like were inside of a tube or something," Stratton recalled. Realizing the peril, Stratton tried to hide beneath the equipment to avoid the flames, but the fire came in, and he was burned. He stayed inside for a bit rather than going outside onto the platform; several others jumped out, and Stratton never saw them again.

When the fire died down some, he went out to the platform where a sea breeze blew the smoke away. It was impossible to lay down or sit down because everything on the deck was hot. He was in pain from the burns; his legs were burned from his thighs to his ankles. His tee-shirt had caught fire; his back, arms, and left side were badly burned. His face was burned. A section of his ear was gone. The hair on his head had burned away.

Thinking back years later on what he saw, Stratton said, "That was so terrible I don't even want to say anything about it." The attack on the *Arizona* cost 1,177 men their lives. Stratton was one of the few survivors, but his condition was so perilous that it would have been hard to call him one of the lucky ones.

He was able to escape the ship by getting the attention of an unknown sailor on the *Vestal* who threw Stratton and five others a heaving line so they could pull themselves to safety. As he was ready to flee the doomed ship, Stratton recalled pulling the skin off his arms "like a big long sock" and throwing it on the deck. They were more than 60 feet away from the *Vestal*, and the water below them was afire. He started pulling himself, hand over hand, with those hands raw from the burns. There were only six survivors; two who crossed would die of their wounds later that night. Once aboard the *Vestal*, the *Arizona* survivors huddled together for some time until a shore boat came along. The sailors had to get up on the dock, reaching and grabbing with their burned hands in order to get ashore, where they were put in an open-air truck and taken to the naval hospital.

The staff at the hospital was well organized despite the chaos of the attack. There, they examined Stratton and discovered that more than 70% of his body had been burned. Because the burns were so bad, the nurses and orderlies couldn't tell which sailors had been given morphine and who hadn't, so the nurses marked an X on the sailors after the shots had been administered, including the time the shot had been given.

The hospital staff doubted that Stratton would survive the trip to the States for treatment, but Stratton insisted that he could make it. In order to convince them that he was able to survive the journey, Stratton stood up while his linens were changed. He didn't get up for a long time after that, but he was sent to the burn unit at the Mare Island Naval Hospital in California, arriving on Christmas Day. Treatment included a lot of antibiotics. When it was time to give him saltwater baths, double sheets were placed beneath him. Four corpsmen would each take a corner of the sheets and would lower him into a tub filled with saltwater. It was rough, but it seemed to help. Stratton's wounds were so bad that the couldn't feed himself or move. A canopy over his bed kept him warm, but he had no sheets or blankets so that the burns were exposed to the open air. He was in the burn unit for nine months. When he was transferred to a hotel that had been taken over by the Navy for the convalescence of the sailors, he weighed 92 pounds. On the morning of the attack, he had weighed around 165 pounds.

He was medically discharged in September 1942. After returning home with his left side disabled, his physical condition improved after a year, so he decided to return to the Navy. There wasn't a lot of opportunity at home or a lot of jobs. Besides, Stratton admits that revenge may have been a motive. The only way to manage his return was through the draft. He had friends on the draft board, and they got him back into the Navy. He went to boot camp in 1944, did well, and was assigned to the USS *Stack*, a destroyer, as a gunner's mate third class. En route to the

Stack's destination, the ship stopped at Pearl Harbor, a customary stop for ships fighting in the Pacific. Stratton remembered tears coming to his eyes as he remembered the events of December 7.

His new assignment would take him to the Pacific, where he would be part of the invasions of New Guinea, the Philippines, and Okinawa. It would not be an easy assignment; there was one night when several destroyers were struck by the Japanese. When Stratton was discharged on December 4, 1945, he realized that it was time to get out of the Navy and move on.

Stratton, although he held no animosity toward the Japanese people, could not shake hands with Japanese pilots during reunions after the war. "You have to understand my position. There's a thousand men down on that ship that I was on and I'm sure they wouldn't do that, and I'm sure they wouldn't want me to do it. I know that I'm very fortunate to be here. I just can't help but think people should be more aware of what happened that day and how many lives were taken. How many of those sailors and Marines on board that ship right now don't even know what happened to them or why it happened or who it was? It seems like an awful, awful waste of life for something that people are going to forget about. We have so many people [today] who don't appreciate their liberty and wouldn't fight for it."

Conclusion

The American war with Japan that began at Pearl Harbor ended at Nagasaki when the United States dropped a second atomic bomb upon the civilian population. But before that grim resolution in 1945, the Japanese were initially able to exploit their success following the attack on Pearl Harbor.

Not long after the attack, the Japanese controlled much of the Pacific including the Philippines, Burma, Dutch East Indies, Singapore, Hong Kong, Wake Island, and Guam. But within six months, the tide was slowly beginning to turn. That turning point was the Battle of Midway, fought from June 4 to 7, 1942. Described by military historian John Keegan as "the most stunning and decisive blow in the history of naval warfare," the engagement of the Americans at Midway was part of Japan's effort to trap U.S. aircraft carriers and, by achieving victory, extending Japan's defenses. The Japanese went to Midway in response to the raid that Lieutenant Colonel James Doolittle had flown over Tokyo. The raid did little damage except to Japan's martial pride and, convinced that the raid had been launched from Midway Island, the Japanese intended to teach the Americans a lesson. But the U.S. Navy had discerned the time and place for the attack and was not surprised when it came. All four of Japan's aircraft carriers were sunk. It was not as easy for Japan to replace its lost aircraft carriers and pilots as it was for the Americans.

By 1945, the war against Japan had come down to the Battle of Iwo Jima and Okinawa. Iwo Jima, considered the fiercest battle in the Pacific Theater, saw the U.S. Marines sustain casualties to approximately 33% of their fighting force. During the 82-day Battle of Okinawa, the Americans lost more than 50,000 troops. Bad as that was, it was worse for the Japanese, who lost 100,000 troops. By July 1945, 64 of Japan's cities had been greatly or partially destroyed by bombing. The Japanese military was nearly impotent, and the country was almost out of oil. Food shortages loomed. The Japanese people were suffering and tired of war. But when the Potsdam Declaration required unconditional surrender from Japan, the Japanese refused. It seemed as though the Japanese would go on fighting even in the face of defeat.

The United States had a second, secret option to end the war. Since 1940, after a warning by Albert Einstein that the Nazis were researching nuclear weapons, the Americans had been developing an atomic weapon. Military advisors had warned President Harry Truman that if American forces invaded Japan, the American casualties would be terrible. Therefore, Truman made the decision to unleash the most terrible weapon the world had ever known.

On August 6, 1945, the Enola Gay flew over Hiroshima and dropped a five-ton bomb on the city. The blast, the equivalent to 15,000 tons of TNT, instantly killed 80,000 people and destroyed four square miles of the city.

Fourteen-year-old Tomiko Matsumoto was late for school and was running to catch up to the other students who were already in line. "I felt as if the sun had dropped on me. Then the blast, strong blast, attacked me. I was under the rubble of the school. I was in the darkness. I couldn't see anything. No one was there. About 320 girls and ten teachers were on the playground but there was nobody . . . my skin was peeling off and hanging down from my neck and then my clothes. My back was burnt. Pieces of glass were speared into my head." Tomiko was picked up by the military and, along with other survivors, taken to shelter. There she saw some of her classmates and a teacher. But by the following morning, she was the only one of her schoolmates who was still alive. During the following weeks, thousands more died, victims of radiation poisoning and wounds.

Japan would not surrender. On August 9, the Americans dropped a second bomb, this one on Nagasaki. Almost 40,000 people died. On August 15, Japan surrendered unconditionally. General Douglas MacArthur, appointed as supreme commander of the Allied Powers arrived in Tokyo on August 30, and on September 2, Japan signed the terms of surrender aboard the USS *Missouri*. MacArthur was in charge of the occupation of Japan with the intention of transforming the country into a democratic nation. But first, the starving Japanese needed food. With the cities in ruins and the government in a state of collapse, Japan needed immediate relief. MacArthur set up a food distribution network.

Then MacArthur, who refused to allow Emperor Hirohito to be tried as a war criminal, obtained the monarch's good will and set about the goal of rebuilding the nation's political structure. The occupation ended on September 8, 1951. Japan was once again in charge of its own sovereignty.

The United States would be forever changed by its role in World War II. The isolationist nation that had existed before December 7, 1941, would emerge as a powerful world leader, its might undiminished by World War II. A new enemy would appear as the Soviet Union, and communism became the bitter foe of the Americans. Japan would become an American ally. The two nations, each having inflicted a deadly surprise attack on the other, would find common ground in the post-war years, growing through alliances in trade and a shared sense of partnership.

But even with the passage of time, the memory of the 1,177 who died on the USS *Arizona* did not fade. In 1962, the USS Arizona Memorial was built to commemorate the sacrifice of the sailors who died upon the ship when the Japanese attacked Pearl Harbor. The memorial is above the sunken hull of the ship. The memorial attracts two million visitors a year who come to pay their respects to those who died.

Respects are also due to those who survived. Donald Stratton was one of the survivors. As the USS *Arizona* was sinking, he and five others aboard the death ship were rescued by a young sailor who risked his own life to save them. Joe George was the sailor, and his military record confirmed his action. But because there was no eyewitness account of what he had done, and no senior officer on his ship, the USS *Vestal*, he could not be awarded a medal. There seemed to be another problem; George had been ordered to cut the line connecting his ship with the burning battleship. Disregarding the order, he threw a line to the six surviving sailors instead of casting off as he had been told to do.

Randy Stratton, Donald Stratton's son, knew the story of his father's rescue, and he was convinced that Joe George, who died in 1996, should get a medal for his deed. Randy Stratton got in touch with George's widow and promised the family that he would do his best to see that their father and husband was recognized for his bravery. Letters to politicians, contact with other Pearl Harbor survivors, and telephone calls to anyone who would listen were all part of his campaign. He enlisted the political influence of Arkansas Senator Tom Cotton, Colorado Senator Cory Gardner, and Arizona Senator Jeff Flake. The Navy found the logbook that had belonged to George; the record included the commendation he received for saving the six sailors who would have died had he not thrown them a line. There was no reason now to deny the dead hero a posthumous medal.

On December 7, 2017, Joe George was awarded the Bronze Star for Valor. The ceremony took place aboard the USS Arizona Memorial. His daughter, Joe Ann Taylor, received the medal for her father. Attending the ceremony were 95-year-old Donald Stratton and Lou Conter, aged 96 and also one of the survivors of the USS *Arizona*. For these men and the others who died on that infamous day, the history was personal. The same was true for the Japanese who perished on August 6 and August 9 when the United States dropped atomic bombs on Hiroshima and Nagasaki.

For the United States and Japan, the war in the Pacific was bookended by the two surprise attacks, the first on Pearl Harbor and the second with atomic bombs on Japan, which sent the two nations on a perilous journey that neither country can ever forget.

Made in the USA
Las Vegas, NV
01 December 2024